HAWAII RULES OF EVIDENCE
2018 Edition

Updated through January 1, 2018

Michigan Legal Publishing Ltd.
QUICK DESK REFERENCE SERIES™

WE WELCOME YOUR FEEDBACK: info@michlp.com

ISBN-13: 978-1-64002-037-5

Table of Contents

Article I - General Provisions

Rule 100. Title and citation.

These rules shall be known and cited as the Hawaii Rules of Evidence. Each rule shall be cited by its number. A complete citation to a rule may read as follows: Rule ___, Hawaii Rules of Evidence, Chapter 626, Hawaii Revised Statutes.

Rule 101. Scope.

These rules govern proceedings in the courts of the State of Hawaii, to the extent and with the exceptions stated in rule 1101.

Rule 102. Purpose and construction.

These rules shall be construed to secure fairness in administration, elimination of unjustifiable expense and delay, and promotion of growth and development of the law of evidence to the end that the truth may be ascertained and proceedings justly determined.

Rule 102.1. Effect of commentary.

The commentary to these rules when published may be used as an aid in understanding the rules, but not as evidence of legislative intent.

Rule 103. Rulings on evidence.

(a) **Effect of erroneous ruling**. Error may not be predicated upon a ruling which admits or excludes evidence unless a substantial right of the party is affected, and:
    (1) *Objection*. In case the ruling is one admitting evidence, a timely objection or motion to strike appears of record, stating the specific ground of objection, if the specific ground was not apparent from the context; or
    (2) *Offer of proof*. In case the ruling is one excluding evidence, the substance of the evidence was made known to the court by offer or was apparent from the context within which questions were asked.
Once the court makes a definitive ruling on the record admitting or excluding evidence, either at or before trial, a party need not renew an objection or offer of proof to preserve a claim of error for appeal.
(b) **Record of offer and ruling**. The court may add any other or further statement which shows the character of the evidence, the form in

which it was offered, the objection made, and the ruling thereon. It may direct the making of an offer in question and answer form.

(c) **Hearing of jury**. In jury cases, proceedings shall be conducted, to the extent practicable, so as to prevent inadmissible evidence from being suggested to the jury by any means, such as making statements or offers of proof or asking questions in the hearing of the jury.

(d) **Plain error**. Nothing in this rule precludes taking notice of plain errors affecting substantial rights although they were not brought to the attention of the court.

Rule 104. Preliminary questions.

(a) **Questions of admissibility generally**. Preliminary questions concerning the qualification of a person to be a witness, the existence of a privilege, or the admissibility of evidence shall be determined by the court, subject to the provisions of subsection (b). In making its determination the court is not bound by the rules of evidence except those with respect to privileges.

(b) **Relevancy conditioned on fact**. When the relevancy of evidence depends upon the fulfillment of a condition of fact, the court shall admit it upon, or subject to, the introduction of evidence sufficient to support a finding of the fulfillment of the condition.

(c) **Hearing of jury**. Hearings on the admissibility of confessions shall in all cases be conducted out of the hearing of the jury. Hearings on other preliminary matters shall be so conducted when the interests of justice require or, when an accused is a witness, if the accused so requests.

(d) **Testimony by accused**. The accused does not, by testifying upon a preliminary matter, subject oneself to cross-examination as to other issues in the case.

(e) **Weight and credibility**. This rule does not limit the right of a party to introduce before the jury evidence relevant to weight or credibility.

Rule 105. Limited admissibility.

When evidence which is admissible as to one party or for one purpose but not admissible as to another party or for another purpose is admitted, the court, upon request, shall restrict the evidence to its proper scope and instruct the jury accordingly.

Rule 106. Remainder of or related writings or recorded statements.

When a writing or recorded statement or part thereof is introduced by a party, an adverse party may require the party at that time to introduce any other part or any other writing or recorded statement which ought in fairness to be considered contemporaneously with it.

Rule 106. Remainder of or related writings or recorded statements.

Article II - Judicial Notice

Rule 201. Judicial notice of adjudicative facts.

(a) **Scope of rule**. This rule governs only judicial notice of adjudicative facts.

(b) **Kinds of facts**. A judicially noticed fact must be one not subject to reasonable dispute in that it is either (1) generally known within the territorial jurisdiction of the trial court, or (2) capable of accurate and ready determination by resort to sources whose accuracy cannot reasonably be questioned.

(c) **When discretionary**. A court may take judicial notice, whether requested or not.

(d) **When mandatory**. A court shall take judicial notice if requested by a party and supplied with the necessary information.

(e) **Opportunity to be heard**. A party is entitled upon timely request to an opportunity to be heard as to the propriety of taking judicial notice and the tenor of the matter noticed. In the absence of prior notification, the request may be made after judicial notice has been taken.

(f) **Time of taking notice**. Judicial notice may be taken at any stage of the proceeding.

(g) **Instructing jury**. In a civil proceeding, the court shall instruct the jury to accept as conclusive any fact judicially noticed. In a criminal case, the court shall instruct the jury that it may, but is not required to, accept as conclusive any fact judicially noticed.

Rule 202. Judicial notice of law.

(a) **Scope of rule**. This rule governs only judicial notice of law.

(b) **Mandatory judicial notice of law**. The court shall take judicial notice of (1) the common law, (2) the constitutions and statutes of the United States and of every state, territory, and other jurisdiction of the United States, (3) all rules adopted by the United States Supreme Court or by the Hawaii Supreme Court, and (4) all duly enacted ordinances of cities or counties of this State.

(c) **Optional judicial notice of law**. Upon reasonable notice to adverse parties, a party may request that the court take, and the court may take, judicial notice of (1) all duly adopted federal and state rules of court, (2) all duly published regulations of federal and state agencies, (3) all duly enacted ordinances of municipalities or other governmental subdivisions of other states, (4) any matter of law which would fall within the scope of this subsection or subsection (b) of this rule but for the fact that it has been replaced, superseded, or otherwise rendered no longer in force, and (5) the laws of foreign countries, international law, and maritime law.

(d) **Determination by court**. All determinations of law made pursuant to this rule shall be made by the court and not by the jury, and the court may consider any relevant material or source, including testimony, whether or not submitted by a party or admissible under these rules.

Article III - Presumptions

Rule 301. Definitions.

The following definitions apply under this article:
  (1) "Presumption" is (A) a rebuttable assumption of fact, (B) that the law requires to be made, (C) from another fact or group of facts found or otherwise established in the action.
  (2) The following are not presumptions under this article:
      (A) *Conclusive presumption*. The trier of fact is compelled by law to accept an assumption of fact as conclusive, regardless of the strength of the opposing evidence; or
      (B) *Inference*. The trier of fact may logically and reasonably make an assumption from another fact or group of facts found or otherwise established in the action, but is not required to do so; or
      (C) *Pre-evidentiary assumption*. The trier of fact is compelled by law to accept the assumption as either rebuttable or conclusive without regard to any other fact determination.
  (3) "Burden of producing evidence" means the obligation of a party to introduce evidence of the existence or nonexistence of a relevant fact sufficient to avoid an adverse peremptory finding on that fact.
  (4) "Burden of proof" means the obligation of a party to establish by evidence a requisite degree of belief concerning a relevant fact in the mind of the trier of fact. The burden of proof may require a party to establish the existence or nonexistence of a fact by a preponderance of the evidence or by clear and convincing proof.

Rule 302. Presumptions in civil proceedings.

(a) **General rule**. In all civil proceedings not otherwise provided for by statute or by these rules, a presumption imposes on the party against whom it is directed either (1) the burden of producing evidence, or (2) the burden of proof.

(b) **Inconsistent presumptions**. If two presumptions are mutually inconsistent, the presumption applies that is founded upon weightier considerations of policy and logic. If considerations of policy and logic are of equal weight neither presumption applies.

(c) **Applicability of federal law**. In all civil proceedings, the effect of a presumption respecting a fact which is an element of a claim or

defense as to which federal law supplies the rule of decision is
determined in accordance with federal law.

Rule 303. Presumptions imposing burden of producing evidence.

(a) **General rule**. A presumption established to implement no public
policy other than to facilitate the determination of the particular
action in which the presumption is applied imposes on the party
against whom it is directed the burden of producing evidence.

(b) **Effect**. The effect of a presumption imposing the burden of
producing evidence is to require the trier of fact to assume the
existence of the presumed fact unless and until evidence is
introduced which would support a finding of its nonexistence, in
which case no instruction on presumption shall be given and the
trier of fact shall determine the existence or nonexistence of the
presumed fact from the evidence and without regard to the
presumption. Nothing in this rule shall be construed to prevent the
drawing of any inferences.

(c) **Presumptions**. The following presumptions, and all other
presumptions established by law that fall within the criteria of
subsection (a) of this rule, are presumptions imposing the burden of
producing evidence:

    (1)   *Money delivered by one to another*. Money delivered by one
to another is presumed to have been due to the latter;

    (2)   *Thing delivered by one to another*. A thing delivered by one
to another is presumed to have belonged to the latter;

    (3)   *Obligation delivered up to the debtor*. An obligation
delivered up to the debtor is presumed to have been paid;

    (4)   *Obligation possessed by creditor*. An obligation possessed
by a creditor is presumed not to have been paid;

    (5)   *Payment of earlier rent or installments*. The payment of
earlier rent or installments is presumed from a receipt for
later rent or installments;

    (6)   *Things possessed*. The things that a person possesses are
presumed to be owned by the person;

    (7)   *Exercise of act of ownership*. A person who exercises acts of
ownership over property is presumed to be the owner of it;

    (8)   *Judgment determines, sets forth rights of parties*. A
judgment, when not conclusive, is presumed to correctly
determine or set forth the rights of the parties, but there is no
presumption that the facts essential to the judgment have
been correctly determined;

    (9)   *Writing*. A writing is presumed to have been truly dated;

(10) *Letter properly addressed and mailed.* A letter correctly addressed and properly mailed is presumed to have been received in the ordinary course of mail;

(11) *Trustee's conveyance to a particular person.* A trustee or other person, whose duty it was to convey real property to a particular person, is presumed to have actually conveyed the real property to the person when such presumption is necessary to perfect title of such person or the person's successor in interest;

(12) *Ancient document affecting real or personal property interest.* A deed or will or other writing purporting to create, terminate, or affect an interest in real or personal property is presumed authentic if:

    (A) It is at least twenty years old;

    (B) It is in such condition as to create no reasonable suspicion concerning its authenticity;

    (C) It was kept, or if found was found, in a place where such writing, if authentic, would be likely to be kept or found; and

    (D) Persons having an interest in the matter have been generally acting as if it were authentic;

(13) *Book or other material purporting to be published by public authority.* A book or other material purporting to be printed, published, or posted to an internet website by public authority is presumed to have been so printed, published, or posted;

(14) *Book or internet website purporting to contain reports of adjudged cases.* A book or government website purporting to contain reports of cases adjudged in the tribunals of the state or nation where the book is published or from which the government website is maintained is presumed to contain correct reports of such cases;

(15) *Continuation of a fact, condition, or state.* A fact, condition, or state of things is presumed to continue; and

(16) *Paid bills.* A bill for goods or services that has been paid is presumed to be authentic and to embody fair and reasonable charges for the itemized goods or services.

Rule 304. Presumptions imposing burden of proof.

(a) **General rule**. A presumption established to implement a public policy other than, or in addition to, facilitating the determination of the particular action in which the presumption is applied imposes on the party against whom it is directed the burden of proof.

(b) **Effect**. The effect of a presumption imposing the burden of proof is to require the trier of fact to assume the existence of the presumed fact unless and until evidence is introduced sufficient to convince the trier of fact of the nonexistence of the presumed fact. Except as otherwise provided by law or by these rules, proof by a preponderance of the evidence is necessary and sufficient to rebut a presumption established under this rule.

(c) **Presumptions**. The following presumptions, and all other presumptions established by law that fall within the criteria of subsection (a) of this rule, are presumptions imposing the burden of proof.

    (1) *Owner of legal title is owner of beneficial title.* The owner of the legal title to property is presumed to be the owner of the full beneficial title. This presumption may be rebutted only by clear and convincing proof.

    (2) *Official duty regularly performed; lawful arrest.* It is presumed that official duty has been regularly performed. This presumption does not apply on an issue as to the lawfulness of an arrest if it is found or otherwise established that the arrest was made without a warrant.

    (3) *Intention of ordinary consequences of voluntary act.* A person is presumed to intend the ordinary consequences of the person's voluntary act.

    (4) *Doing of an unlawful act.* An unlawful intent is presumed from the doing of an unlawful act.

    (5) *Any court, any judge acting as such.* Any court of this State or the United States, or any court of general jurisdiction in any other state or nation, or any judge of such a court, acting as such, is presumed to have acted in the lawful exercise of its jurisdiction. This presumption applies only when the act of the court or judge is under collateral attack.

    (6) *Ceremonial marriage.* A ceremonial marriage is presumed to be valid.

    (7) Death. A person who is absent for a continuous period of five years, during which the person has not been heard from, and whose absence is not satisfactorily explained after diligent search or inquiry, is presumed to be dead.

Rule 305. Prima facie evidence.

A statute providing that a fact or a group of facts is prima facie evidence of another fact establishes a presumption within the meaning of this article unless the statute expressly provides that such prima facie evidence is conclusive.

Rule 306. Presumptions in criminal proceedings.

(a) **Presumptions against the accused**.

  (1) *Scope*. Except as otherwise provided by statute, in criminal proceedings, presumptions against an accused, recognized at common law or created by statute, including statutory provisions that certain facts are prima facie evidence of other facts or of guilt, are governed by this subsection.

  (2) *Submission to jury*. When a presumed fact establishes an element of the offense or negatives a defense, the court may submit the presumption to the jury only if a reasonable juror on the evidence as a whole, including the evidence of the basic facts, could find the presumed fact beyond a reasonable doubt.

  (3) *Instructing the jury*. The court may not direct the jury to find a presumed fact against the accused. Whenever a presumption against the accused is submitted to the jury, the court shall instruct the jury that, if it finds the basic facts beyond a reasonable doubt, it may infer the presumed fact but is not required to do so. In addition, if the presumed fact establishes an element of the offense or negatives a defense, the court shall instruct the jury that its existence, on all the evidence, must be proved beyond a reasonable doubt.

(b) **Presumptions against the State**. Except as otherwise provided by statute, in criminal proceedings, presumptions against the State, recognized at common law or created by statute, impose on the State either (1) the burden of producing evidence, or (2) the burden of proof.

(c) **Inconsistent presumptions**. If two presumptions are mutually inconsistent, the presumption applies that is founded upon weightier considerations of policy and logic. If considerations of policy and logic are of equal weight, neither presumption applies.

Rule 306. Presumptions in criminal proceedings.

Article IV - Relevancy and its Limits

Rule 401. Definition of "relevant evidence".

"Relevant evidence" means evidence having any tendency to make the existence of any fact that is of consequence to the determination of the action more probable or less probable than it would be without the evidence.

Rule 402. Relevant evidence generally admissible; irrelevant evidence inadmissible.

All relevant evidence is admissible, except as otherwise provided by the Constitutions of the United States and the State of Hawaii, by statute, by these rules, or by other rules adopted by the supreme court. Evidence which is not relevant is not admissible.

Rule 403. Exclusion of relevant evidence on grounds of prejudice, confusion, or waste of time.

Although relevant, evidence may be excluded if its probative value is substantially outweighed by the danger of unfair prejudice, confusion of the issues, or misleading the jury, or by considerations of undue delay, waste of time, or needless presentation of cumulative evidence.

Rule 404. Character evidence not admissible to prove conduct; exceptions; other crimes.

(a) **Character evidence generally**. Evidence of a person's character or a trait of a person's character is not admissible for the purpose of proving action in conformity therewith on a particular occasion, except:

    (1) *Character of accused*. Evidence of a pertinent trait of character of an accused offered by an accused, or by the prosecution to rebut the same;

    (2) *Character of victim*. Evidence of a pertinent trait of character of the victim of the crime offered by an accused, or by the prosecution to rebut the same, or evidence of a character trait of peacefulness of the victim offered by the prosecution in a homicide case to rebut evidence that the victim was the first aggressor;

    (3) *Character of witness*. Evidence of the character of a witness, as provided in rules 607, 608, 609, and 609.1.

(b) **Other crimes, wrongs, or acts**. Evidence of other crimes, wrongs, or acts is not admissible to prove the character of a person in order to show action in conformity therewith. It may, however, be admissible where such evidence is probative of another fact that is of consequence to the determination of the action, such as proof of motive, opportunity, intent, preparation, plan, knowledge, identity, modus operandi, or absence of mistake or accident. In criminal cases, the proponent of evidence to be offered under this subsection shall provide reasonable notice in advance of trial, or during trial if the court excuses pretrial notice on good cause shown, of the date, location, and general nature of any such evidence it intends to introduce at trial.

Rule 405. Methods of proving character.

(a) **Reputation or opinion**. In all cases in which evidence of character or a trait of character of a person is admissible, proof may be made by testimony as to reputation or by testimony in the form of an opinion. On cross-examination, inquiry is allowable into relevant specific instances of conduct.

(b) **Specific instances of conduct**. In cases in which character or a trait of character of a person is an essential element of a charge, claim, or defense, proof may also be made of specific instances of the person's conduct.

Rule 406. Habit; routine practice.

Evidence of the habit of a person or of the routine practice of an organization, whether corroborated or not and regardless of the presence of eyewitnesses, is relevant to prove that the conduct of the person or organization on a particular occasion was in conformity with the habit or routine practice.

Rule 407. Subsequent remedial measures.

When, after an event, measures are taken which, if taken previously, would have made the event less likely to occur, evidence of the subsequent measures is not admissible to prove negligence or culpable conduct in connection with the event. This rule does not require the exclusion of evidence of subsequent measures when offered for another purpose, such as proving dangerous defect in products liability cases, ownership, control, or feasibility of precautionary measures, if controverted, or impeachment.

Rule 408. Compromise, offers to compromise, and mediation proceedings.

Evidence of (1) furnishing or offering or promising to furnish, or (2) accepting or offering or promising to accept, a valuable consideration in compromising or attempting to compromise a claim which was disputed as to either validity or amount, or (3) mediation or attempts to mediate a claim which was disputed, is not admissible to prove liability for or invalidity of the claim or its amount. Evidence of conduct or statements made in compromise negotiations or mediation proceedings is likewise not admissible. This rule does not require the exclusion of any evidence otherwise discoverable merely because it is presented in the course of compromise negotiations or mediation proceedings. This rule also does not require exclusion when the evidence is offered for another purpose, such as proving bias or prejudice of a witness, negativing a contention of undue delay, or proving an effort to obstruct a criminal investigation or prosecution.

Rule 409. Payment of medical and similar expenses.

Evidence of furnishing or offering or promising to pay medical, hospital, or similar expenses occasioned by an injury is not admissible to prove liability for the injury.

Rule 409.5. Admissibility of expressions of sympathy and condolence.

Evidence of statements or gestures that express sympathy, commiseration, or condolence concerning the consequences of an event in which the declarant was a participant is not admissible to prove liability for any claim growing out of the event. This rule does not require the exclusion of an apology or other statement that acknowledges or implies fault even though contained in, or part of, any statement or gesture excludable under this rule.

Rule 410. Inadmissibility of pleas, plea discussions, and related statements.

Except as otherwise provided in this rule, evidence of the following is not, in any civil or criminal proceeding, admissible against the defendant who made the plea or was a participant in the plea discussions:
  (1)   A plea of guilty which was later withdrawn;
  (2)   A plea of nolo contendere;

(3) Any statement made in the course of any proceedings under Rule 11 of the Hawaii Rules of Penal Procedure or comparable federal or state procedure regarding either of the foregoing pleas; or

(4) Any statements made in the course of plea discussions with an attorney for the prosecuting authority which do not result in a plea of guilty or which result in a plea of guilty later withdrawn.

However, such a statement is admissible (i) in any proceeding wherein another statement made in the course of the same plea or plea discussions has been introduced and the statement ought in fairness be considered contemporaneously with it, or (ii) in a criminal proceeding for perjury or false statement if the statement was made by the defendant under oath, on the record and in the presence of counsel.

Rule 411. Liability insurance.

Evidence that a person was or was not insured against liability is not admissible upon the issue whether the person acted negligently or otherwise wrongfully. This rule does not require the exclusion of evidence of insurance against liability when offered for another purpose, such as proof of agency, ownership, or control, or bias or prejudice of a witness.

Rule 412. Sexual offense and sexual harassment cases; relevance of victim's past behavior.

(a) Notwithstanding any other provision of law, in a criminal case in which a person is accused of a sexual offense, reputation or opinion evidence of the past sexual behavior of an alleged victim of the sexual offense is not admissible to prove the character of the victim to show action in conformity therewith.

(b) Notwithstanding any other provision of law, in a criminal case in which a person is accused of a sexual offense, evidence of an alleged victim's past sexual behavior other than reputation or opinion evidence is not admissible to prove the character of the victim to show action in conformity therewith, unless the evidence is:

    (1) Admitted in accordance with subsection (c)(1) and (2) and is constitutionally required to be admitted; or

    (2) Admitted in accordance with subsection (c) and is evidence of:

        (A) Past sexual behavior with persons other than the accused, offered by the accused upon the issue of whether the accused was or was not, with respect to the alleged victim, the source of semen or injury; or

   (B)   Past sexual behavior with the accused and is offered by the accused upon the issue of whether the alleged victim consented to the sexual behavior with respect to which sexual assault is alleged.

(c)

   (1)   If the person accused of committing a sexual offense intends to offer under subsection (b) evidence of specific instances of the alleged victim's past sexual behavior, the accused shall make a written motion to offer the evidence not later than fifteen days before the date on which the trial in which the evidence is to be offered is scheduled to begin, except that the court may allow the motion to be made at a later date, including during trial, if the court determines either that the evidence is newly discovered and could not have been obtained earlier through the exercise of due diligence or that the issue to which the evidence relates has newly arisen in the case. Any motion made under this paragraph shall be served on all other parties and on the alleged victim.

   (2)   The motion described in paragraph (1) shall be accompanied by a written offer of proof. If the court determines that the offer of proof contains evidence described in subsection (b), the court shall order a hearing in chambers to determine if the evidence is admissible. At the hearing, the parties may call witnesses, including the alleged victim, and offer relevant evidence. Notwithstanding subsection (b) of rule 104, if the relevancy of the evidence that the accused seeks to offer in the trial depends upon the fulfillment of a condition of fact, the court, at the hearing in chambers or at a subsequent hearing in chambers scheduled for this purpose, shall accept evidence on the issue of whether the condition of fact is fulfilled and shall determine the issue.

   (3)   If the court determines on the basis of the hearing described in paragraph (2) that the evidence that the accused seeks to offer is relevant and that the probative value of the evidence outweighs the danger of unfair prejudice, the evidence shall be admissible in the trial to the extent an order made by the court specifies evidence that may be offered and areas with respect to which the alleged victim may be examined or cross-examined.

(d) In any civil action alleging conduct which constitutes a sexual offense or sexual harassment, opinion evidence, reputation evidence, and evidence of specific instances of plaintiff's sexual conduct, or any of such evidence, is not admissible by the defendant to prove consent by the plaintiff or the absence of injury to the plaintiff, unless the injury alleged by the plaintiff is in the nature of loss of consortium.

(e) Subsection (d) shall not be applicable to evidence of the plaintiff's sexual conduct with the alleged perpetrator.

(f) In a civil action alleging conduct which constitutes a sexual offense or sexual harassment, if the plaintiff introduces evidence, including testimony of a witness, or the plaintiff as a witness gives testimony, and the evidence or testimony relates to the plaintiff's sexual conduct, the defendant may cross-examine the witness who gives the testimony and offer relevant evidence limited specifically to the rebuttal of the evidence introduced by the plaintiff or given by the plaintiff.

(g) Nothing in subsections (d), (e) or (f) shall be construed to make inadmissible evidence offered to attack the credibility of the plaintiff.

(h) For purposes of this rule, the term "past sexual behavior" means sexual behavior other than the sexual behavior with respect to which a sexual offense or sexual harassment is alleged.

Article V - Privileges

Rule 501. Privileges recognized only as provided.

Except as otherwise required by the Constitution of the United States, the Constitution of the State of Hawaii, or provided by Act of Congress or Hawaii statute, and except as provided in these rules or in other rules adopted by the Supreme Court of the State of Hawaii, no person has a privilege to:

    (1)   Refuse to be a witness; or
    (2)   Refuse to disclose any matter; or
    (3)   Refuse to produce any object or writing; or
    (4)   Prevent another from being a witness or disclosing any matter or producing any object or writing.

Rule 502. Required reports privileged by statute.

A person, corporation, association, or other organization or entity, either public or private, making a return or report required by law to be made has a privilege to refuse to disclose and to prevent any other person from disclosing the return or report, if the law requiring it to be made so provides. A public officer or agency to whom a return or report is required by law to be made has a privilege to refuse to disclose the return or report if the law requiring it to be made so provides. No privilege exists under this rule in actions involving perjury, false statements, fraud in the return or report, or other failure to comply with the law in question.

Rule 503. Lawyer-client privilege.

(a) **Definitions**. As used in this rule:

    (1)   A "client" is a person, public officer, or corporation, association, or other organization or entity, either public or private, who is rendered professional legal services by a lawyer, or who consults a lawyer with a view to obtaining professional legal services.
    (2)   A "representative of the client" is one having authority to obtain professional legal services, or to act on advice rendered pursuant thereto, on behalf of the client.
    (3)   A "lawyer" is a person authorized, or reasonably believed by the client to be authorized, to practice law in any state or nation.

    (4)   A "representative of the lawyer" is one directed by the lawyer to assist in the rendition of professional legal services.

    (5)   A communication is "confidential" if not intended to be disclosed to third persons other than those to whom disclosure would be in furtherance of the rendition of professional legal services to the client or those reasonably necessary for the transmission of the communication.

(b) **General rule of privilege**. A client has a privilege to refuse to disclose and to prevent any other person from disclosing confidential communications made for the purpose of facilitating the rendition of professional legal services to the client (1) between the client or the client's representative and the lawyer or the lawyer's representative, or (2) between the lawyer and the lawyer's representative, or (3) by the client or the client's representative or the lawyer or a representative of the lawyer to a lawyer or a representative of a lawyer representing another party in a pending action and concerning a matter of common interest, or (4) between representatives of the client or between the client and a representative of the client, or (5) among lawyers and their representatives representing the same client.

(c) **Who may claim the privilege**. The privilege may be claimed by the client, the client's guardian or conservator, the personal representative of a deceased client, or the successor, trustee, or similar representative of a corporation, association, or other organization, whether or not in existence. The person who was the lawyer or the lawyer's representative at the time of the communication shall claim the privilege on behalf of the client unless expressly released by the client.

(d) **Exceptions**. There is no privilege under this rule:

    (1)   *Furtherance of crime or fraud.* If the services of the lawyer were sought, obtained, or used to enable or aid anyone to commit or plan to commit what the client knew or reasonably should have known to be a crime or fraud;

    (2)   *Prevention of crime or fraud.* As to a communication reflecting the client's intent to commit a criminal or fraudulent act that the lawyer reasonably believes is likely to result in death or substantial bodily harm, or in substantial injury to the financial interests or property of another;

    (3)   *Claimants through same deceased client.* As to a communication relevant to an issue between parties who claim through the same deceased client, regardless of

whether the claims are by testate or intestate succession or by inter vivos transaction;

(4) *Breach of duty by lawyer or client.* As to a communication relevant to an issue of breach of duty by the lawyer to the client or by the client to the lawyer;

(5) *Document attested by lawyer.* As to a communication relevant to an issue concerning an attested document to which the lawyer is an attesting witness;

(6) *Joint clients.* As to a communication relevant to a matter of common interest between two or more clients if the communication was made by any of them to a lawyer retained or consulted in common, when offered in an action between any of the clients; or

(7) *Lawyer's professional responsibility.* As to a communication the disclosure of which is required or authorized by the Hawaii rules of professional conduct for attorneys.

Rule 504. Physician-patient privilege.

(a) **Definitions**. As used in this rule:

(1) A "patient" is a person who consults or is examined or interviewed by a physician.

(2) A "physician" is a person authorized, or reasonably believed by the patient to be authorized, to practice medicine in any state or nation.

(3) A communication is "confidential" if not intended to be disclosed to third persons other than those present to further the interest of the patient in the consultation, examination, or interview, or persons reasonably necessary for the transmission of the communication, or persons who are participating in the diagnosis and treatment under the direction of the physician, including members of the patient's family.

(b) **General rule of privilege**. A patient has a privilege to refuse to disclose and to prevent any other person from disclosing confidential communications made for the purpose of diagnosis or treatment of the patient's physical, mental, or emotional condition, including alcohol or drug addiction, among oneself, the patient's physician, and persons who are participating in the diagnosis or treatment under the direction of the physician, including members of the patient's family.

(c) **Who may claim the privilege**. The privilege may be claimed by the patient, the patient's guardian or conservator, or the personal representative of a deceased patient. The person who was the physician at the time of the communication is presumed to have authority to claim the privilege but only on behalf of the patient.

(d) **Exceptions**.

    (1) *Proceedings for hospitalization.* There is no privilege under this rule for communications relevant to an issue in proceedings to hospitalize the patient for mental illness or substance abuse, or in proceedings for the discharge or release of a patient previously hospitalized for mental illness or substance abuse.

    (2) *Examination by order of court.* If the court orders an examination of the physical, mental, or emotional condition of a patient, whether a party or a witness, communications made in the course thereof are not privileged under this rule with respect to the particular purpose for which the examination is ordered unless the court orders otherwise.

    (3) *Condition an element of claim or defense.* There is no privilege under this rule as to a communication relevant to the physical, mental, or emotional condition of the patient in any proceeding in which the patient relies upon the condition as an element of the patient's claim or defense or, after the patient's death, in any proceeding in which any party relies upon the condition as an element of the party's claim or defense.

    (4) *Proceedings against physician.* There is no privilege under this rule in any administrative or judicial proceeding in which the competency, practitioner's license, or practice of the physician is at issue, provided that the identifying data of the patients whose records are admitted into evidence shall be kept confidential unless waived by the patient. The administrative agency, board, or commission may close the proceeding to the public to protect the confidentiality of the patient.

    (5) *Furtherance of crime or tort.* There is no privilege under this rule if the services of the physician were sought, obtained, or used to enable or aid anyone to commit or plan to commit what the patient knew or reasonably should have known to be a crime or tort.

    (6) *Prevention of crime or tort.* There is no privilege under this rule as to a communication reflecting the patient's intent to commit a criminal or tortious act that the physician reasonably believes is likely to result in death or substantial bodily harm.

Rule 504.1. Psychologist-client privilege.

(a) **Definitions**. As used in this rule:
  (1) A "client" is a person who consults or is examined or interviewed by a psychologist.
  (2) A "psychologist" is a person authorized, or reasonably believed by the client to be authorized, to engage in the diagnosis or treatment of a mental or emotional condition, including substance addiction or abuse.
  (3) A communication is "confidential" if not intended to be disclosed to third persons other than those present to further the interest of the client in the consultation, examination, or interview, or persons reasonably necessary for the transmission of the communication, or persons who are participating in the diagnosis or treatment of the client's mental or emotional condition under the direction of the psychologist, including members of the client's family.

(b) **General rule of privilege**. A client has a privilege to refuse to disclose and to prevent any other person from disclosing confidential communications made for the purpose of diagnosis or treatment of the client's mental or emotional condition, including substance addiction or abuse, among the client, the client's psychologist, and persons who are participating in the diagnosis or treatment under the direction of the psychologist, including members of the client's family.

(c) **Who may claim the privilege**. The privilege may be claimed by the client, the client's guardian or conservator, or the personal representative of a deceased client. The person who was the psychologist at the time of the communication is presumed to have authority to claim the privilege but only on behalf of the client.

(d) **Exceptions**.
  (1) *Proceedings for hospitalization.* There is no privilege under this rule for communications relevant to an issue in proceedings to hospitalize the client for mental illness or substance abuse, or in proceedings for the discharge or release of a client previously hospitalized for mental illness or substance abuse.
  (2) *Examination by order of court.* If the court orders an examination of the physical, mental, or emotional condition of a client, whether a party or a witness, communications made in the course thereof are not privileged under this rule with respect to the particular purpose for which the examination is ordered unless the court orders otherwise.

(3) *Condition an element of claim or defense.* There is no privilege under this rule as to a communication relevant to the physical, mental, or emotional condition of the client in any proceeding in which the client relies upon the condition as an element of the client's claim or defense or, after the client's death, in any proceeding in which any party relies upon the condition as an element of the party's claim or defense.

(4) *Proceedings against psychologist.* There is no privilege under this rule in any administrative or judicial proceeding in which the competency, practitioner's license, or practice of the psychologist is at issue, provided that the identifying data of the clients whose records are admitted into evidence shall be kept confidential unless waived by the client. The administrative agency, board, or commission may close the proceeding to the public to protect the confidentiality of the client.

(5) *Furtherance of crime or tort.* There is no privilege under this rule if the services of the psychologist were sought, obtained, or used to enable or aid anyone to commit or plan to commit what the client knew or reasonably should have known to be a crime or tort.

(6) *Prevention of crime or tort.* There is no privilege under this rule as to a communication reflecting the client's intent to commit a criminal or tortious act that the psychologist reasonably believes is likely to result in death or substantial bodily harm.

Rule 505. Spousal privilege.

(a) **Criminal proceedings**. In a criminal proceeding, the spouse of the accused has a privilege not to testify against the accused. This privilege may be claimed only by the spouse who is called to testify.

(b) **Confidential marital communications; all proceedings**.

    (1) *Definition.* A "confidential marital communication" is a private communication between spouses that is not intended for disclosure to any other person.

    (2) Either party to a confidential marital communication has a privilege to refuse to disclose and to prevent any other person from disclosing that communication.

(c) **Exceptions**. There is no privilege under this rule (1) in proceedings in which one spouse is charged with a crime against the person or property of (A) the other, (B) a child of either, (C) a third person residing in the household of either, or (D) a third person committed in the course of committing a crime against any of these, or (2) as to matters occurring prior to the marriage.

Rule 505.5. Victim-counselor privilege.

(a) **Definitions**. As used in this rule:

(1) A communication is "confidential" if not intended to be disclosed to third persons other than those to whom disclosure would be in furtherance of the provision of counseling or treatment services to the victim or those reasonably necessary for the transmission of the communication.

(2) "Domestic violence victims' program" means any refuge, shelter, office, safe home, institution, or center established for the purpose of offering assistance to victims of abuse through crisis intervention, medical, legal, or support counseling.

(3) "Sexual assault crisis center" means any office, institution, or center offering assistance to victims of sexual assault and the families of such victims through crisis intervention, medical, legal, or support counseling.

(4) "Social worker" means a person who has received a master's degree in social work from a school of social work accredited by the Council on Social Work Education.

(5) A "victim" is a person who consults a victim counselor for assistance in overcoming any adverse emotional or psychological effect of sexual assault, domestic violence, or child abuse.

(6) A "victim counseling program" is any activity of a domestic violence victims' program or a sexual assault crisis center that has, as its primary function, the counseling and treatment of sexual assault, domestic violence, or child abuse victims and their families, and that operates independently of any law enforcement agency, prosecutor's office, or the department of human services.

(7) A "victim counselor" is either a sexual assault counselor or a domestic violence victims' counselor. A sexual assault counselor is a person who is employed by or is a volunteer in a sexual assault crisis center, has undergone a minimum of thirty-five hours of training and who is, or who reports to and is under the direct control and supervision of, a social worker, nurse, psychiatrist, psychologist, or psychotherapist, and whose primary function is the rendering of advice,

counseling or assistance to victims of sexual assault. A domestic violence victims' counselor is a person who is employed by or is a volunteer in a domestic violence victims' program, has undergone a minimum of twenty-five hours of training and who is, or who reports to and is under the direct control and supervision of, a direct service supervisor of a domestic violence victims' program, and whose primary function is the rendering of advice, counseling, or assistance to victims of abuse.

(b) **General rule of privilege**. A victim has a privilege to refuse to disclose and to prevent any other person from disclosing confidential communications made to a victim counselor for the purpose of counseling or treatment of the victim for the emotional or psychological effects of sexual assault, domestic violence, or child abuse or neglect, and to refuse to provide evidence that would identify the name, location, or telephone number of a safe house, abuse shelter, or other facility that provided temporary emergency shelter to the victim.

(c) **Who may claim the privilege**. The privilege may be claimed by the victim, the victim's guardian or conservator, or the personal representative of a deceased victim. The person who was the victim counselor at the time of the communication is presumed to have authority to claim the privilege but only on behalf of the victim.

(d) **Exceptions**. There is no privilege under this rule:

    (1) *Perjured testimony by victim.* If the victim counselor reasonably believes that the victim has given perjured testimony and a party to the proceeding has made an offer of proof that perjury may have been committed.

    (2) *Physical appearance and condition of victim.* In matters of proof concerning the physical appearance and condition of the victim at the time of the alleged crime.

    (3) *Breach of duty by victim counselor or victim counseling program.* As to a communication relevant to an issue of breach of duty by the victim counselor or victim counseling program to the victim.

    (4) *Mandatory reporting.* To relieve victim counselors of any duty to refuse to report child abuse or neglect under chapter 350, domestic abuse under chapter 586, or abuse of a vulnerable adult under part X of chapter 346, and to refuse to provide evidence in child abuse proceedings under chapter 587A.

    (5) *Proceedings for hospitalization.* For communications relevant to an issue in proceedings to hospitalize the victim

for mental illness or substance abuse, or in proceedings for the discharge or release of a victim previously hospitalized for mental illness or substance abuse.

(6) *Examination by order of court.* If the court orders an examination of the physical, mental, or emotional condition of a victim, whether a party or a witness, communications made in the course thereof are not privileged under this rule with respect to the particular purpose of which the examination is ordered unless the court orders otherwise.

(7) *Condition an element of claim or defense.* As to a communication relevant to the physical, mental, or emotional condition of the victim in any proceeding in which the victim relies upon the condition as an element of the victim's claim or defense or, after the victim's death, in any proceeding in which any party relies upon the condition as an element of the party's claim or defense.

(8) *Proceedings against the victim counselor.* In any administrative or judicial proceeding in which the competency or practice of the victim counselor or of the victim counseling program is at issue, provided that the identifying data of the victims whose records are admitted into evidence shall be kept confidential unless waived by the victim. The administrative agency, board or commission shall close to the public any portion of a proceeding, as necessary to protect the confidentiality of the victim.

Rule 506. Communications to clergy.

(a) **Definitions**. As used in this rule:
   (1) A "member of the clergy" is a minister, priest, rabbi, Christian Science practitioner, or other similar functionary of a religious organization, or an individual reasonably believed so to be by the communicant.
   (2) A communication is "confidential" if made privately and not intended for further disclosure except to other persons present in furtherance of the purpose of the communication.

(b) **General rule of privilege**. A person has a privilege to refuse to disclose and to prevent another from disclosing a confidential communication by the person to a member of the clergy in the latter's professional character as spiritual advisor.

(c) **Who may claim the privilege**. The privilege may be claimed by the communicant or by the communicant's guardian, conservator, or personal representative. The member of the clergy may claim the privilege on behalf of the communicant. Authority so to do is presumed in the absence of evidence to the contrary.

Rule 507. Political vote.

Every person has a privilege to refuse to disclose the tenor of the person's vote at a political election conducted pursuant to chapter 11, by secret ballot unless the vote was cast illegally.

Rule 508. Trade secrets.

A person has a privilege, which may be claimed by the person or the person's agent or employee, to refuse to disclose and to prevent other persons from disclosing a trade secret owned by the person, if allowance of the privilege will not tend to conceal fraud or otherwise work injustice. When disclosure is directed, the judge shall take such protective measure as the interests of the holder of the privilege and of the parties and the furtherance of justice may require.

Rule 509. Privilege against self-incrimination.

To the extent that such privilege exists under the Constitution of the United States or the State of Hawaii, a person has a privilege to refuse to disclose any matter that may tend to incriminate the person.

Rule 510. Identity of informer.

(a) **Rule of privilege**. The government or a state or subdivision thereof has a privilege to refuse to disclose the identity of a person who has furnished information relating to or assisting in an investigation of a possible violation of law to a law enforcement officer or member of a legislative committee or its staff conducting an investigation.

(b) **Who may claim**. The privilege may be claimed by an appropriate representative of the government, regardless of whether the information was furnished to an officer of the government or of a state or subdivision thereof. The privilege may be claimed by an appropriate representative of a state or subdivision if the information was furnished to an officer thereof, except that in criminal cases the privilege shall not be allowed if the government objects.

(c) **Exceptions**.

(1) *Voluntary disclosure; informer a witness*. No privilege exists under this rule if the identity of the informer or the informer's interest in the subject matter of the informer's communication has been disclosed to those who would have

cause to resent the communication by a holder of the privilege or by the informer's own action, or if the informer appears as a witness for the government.

(2) *Testimony on merits.* If it appears from the evidence in the case or from other showing by a party that an informer may be able to give testimony necessary to a fair determination of the issue of guilt or innocence in a criminal case or of a material issue on the merits in a civil case to which the government is a party, and the government invokes the privilege, the judge shall give the government an opportunity to show in camera facts relevant to determining whether the informer can, in fact, supply that testimony. The showing will ordinarily be in the form of affidavits, but the judge may direct that testimony be taken if the judge finds that the matter cannot be resolved satisfactorily upon affidavit. If the judge finds that there is a reasonable probability that the informer can give the testimony, and the government elects not to disclose the informer's identity, the judge on motion of the defendant in a criminal case shall dismiss the charges to which the testimony would relate, and the judge may do so on the judge's own motion. In civil cases, the judge may make any order that justice requires. Evidence submitted to the judge shall be sealed and preserved to be made available to the appellate court in the event of an appeal, and the contents shall not otherwise be revealed without consent of the government. All counsel and parties shall be permitted to be present at every stage of proceedings under this paragraph except a showing in camera, at which no counsel or party shall be permitted to be present.

(3) *Legality of obtaining evidence.* If information from an informer is relied upon to establish the legality of the means by which evidence was obtained and the judge is not satisfied that the information was received from an informer reasonably believed to be reliable or credible, the judge may require the identity of the informer to be disclosed. The judge shall, on request of the government, direct that the disclosure be made in camera. All counsel and parties concerned with the issue of legality shall be permitted to be present at every stage of proceedings under this paragraph except a disclosure in camera, at which no counsel or party shall be permitted to be present. If disclosure of the identity of the informer is made in camera, the record thereof shall be sealed and preserved to be made available to the appellate

court in the event of an appeal, and the contents shall not otherwise be revealed without consent of the government.

Rule 511. Waiver of privilege by voluntary disclosure.

A person upon whom these rules confer a privilege against disclosure waives the privilege if, while holder of the privilege, the person or the person's predecessor voluntarily discloses or consents to disclosure of any significant part of the privileged matter. This rule does not apply if the disclosure itself is a privileged communication.

Rule 512. Privileged matter disclosed under compulsion or without opportunity to claim privilege.

Evidence of a statement or other disclosure of privileged matter is not admissible against the holder of the privilege if the disclosure was (1) compelled erroneously, or (2) made without opportunity to claim the privilege.

Rule 513. Comment upon or inference from claim of privilege; instructions.

(a) **Comment or inference not permitted**. The claim of a privilege, whether in the present proceeding or upon a prior occasion, is not a proper subject of comment by judge or counsel. No inference may be drawn therefrom.

(b) **Claiming privilege without knowledge of jury**. In jury cases, proceedings shall be conducted, to the extent practicable, so as to facilitate the making of claims of privilege without the knowledge of the jury.

(c) **Jury instruction**. Upon request, any party exercising a privilege (1) is entitled to an instruction that no inference may be drawn therefrom, or (2) is entitled to have no instruction on the matter given to the jury. Conflicting requests among multiple parties shall be resolved by the court as justice may require.

Article VI - Witnesses

Rule 601. General rule of competency.

Every person is competent to be a witness except as otherwise provided in these rules.

Rule 602. Lack of personal knowledge.

A witness may not testify to a matter unless evidence is introduced sufficient to support a finding that the witness has personal knowledge of the matter. Evidence to prove personal knowledge may, but need not, consist of the witness' own testimony. This rule is subject to the provisions of rule 703, relating to opinion testimony by expert witnesses.

Rule 603. Oath or affirmation.

Before testifying, every witness shall be required to declare that the witness will testify truthfully, by oath or affirmation administered in a form calculated to awaken the witness' conscience and impress the witness' mind with the witness' duty to do so.

Rule 604. Interpreters.

An interpreter is subject to the provisions of these rules relating to qualification as an expert and the administration of an oath or affirmation that the interpreter will make a true translation.

Rule 605. Competency of judge as witness.

The judge presiding at the trial may not testify in that trial as a witness. No objection need be made in order to preserve the point.

Rule 606. Competency of juror as witness.

(a) **At the trial**. A member of the jury may not testify as a witness before that jury in the trial of the case in which the member is sitting as a juror.
(b) **Inquiry into validity of verdict or indictment**. Upon an inquiry into the validity of a verdict or indictment, a juror may not testify concerning the effect of anything upon the juror's or any other juror's mind or emotions as influencing the juror to assent to or dissent from the verdict or indictment or concerning the juror's mental processes in connection therewith. Nor may the juror's

affidavit or evidence of any statement by the juror indicating an effect of this kind be received.

Rule 607. Who may impeach.

The credibility of a witness may be attacked by any party, including the party calling the witness.

Rule 608. Evidence of character and conduct of witness.

(a) **Opinion and reputation evidence of character**. The credibility of a witness may be attacked or supported by evidence in the form of opinion or reputation, but subject to these limitations:
   (1) The evidence may refer only to character for truthfulness or untruthfulness, and
   (2) Evidence of truthful character is admissible only after the character of the witness for truthfulness has been attacked by opinion or reputation evidence or otherwise.
(b) **Specific instances of conduct**. Specific instances of the conduct of a witness, for the purpose of attacking the witness' credibility, if probative of untruthfulness, may be inquired into on cross-examination of the witness and, in the discretion of the court, may be proved by extrinsic evidence. When a witness testifies to the character of another witness under subsection (a), relevant specific instances of the other witness' conduct may be inquired into on cross-examination but may not be proved by extrinsic evidence.
The giving of testimony, whether by an accused or by any other witness, does not operate as a waiver of the witness' privilege against self-incrimination when examined with respect to matters which relate only to credibility.

Rule 609. Impeachment by evidence of conviction of crime.

(a) **General rule**. For the purpose of attacking the credibility of a witness, evidence that the witness has been convicted of a crime is inadmissible except when the crime is one involving dishonesty. However, in a criminal case where the defendant takes the stand, the defendant shall not be questioned or evidence introduced as to whether the defendant has been convicted of a crime, for the sole purpose of attacking credibility, unless the defendant has oneself introduced testimony for the purpose of establishing the defendant's credibility as a witness, in which case the defendant shall be treated as any other witness as provided in this rule.

(b) **Effect of pardon**. Evidence of a conviction is not admissible under this rule if the conviction has been the subject of a pardon.

(c) **Juvenile convictions**. Evidence of juvenile convictions is admissible to the same extent as are criminal convictions under subsection (a) of this rule.

(d) **Pendency of appeal**. The pendency of an appeal therefrom does not render evidence of a conviction inadmissible. Evidence of the pendency of an appeal is admissible.

Rule 609.1. Evidence of bias, interest, or motive.

(a) **General rule**. The credibility of a witness may be attacked by evidence of bias, interest, or motive.

(b) **Extrinsic evidence of bias, interest, or motive**. Extrinsic evidence of a witness' bias, interest, or motive is not admissible unless, on cross-examination, the matter is brought to the attention of the witness and the witness is afforded an opportunity to explain or deny the matter.

Rule 610. Religious beliefs or opinions.

Evidence of beliefs or opinions of a witness on matters of religion is not admissible for the purpose of showing that by reason of their nature the witness' credibility is impaired or enhanced.

Rule 611. Mode and order of interrogation and presentation.

(a) **Control by court**. The court shall exercise reasonable control over the mode and order of interrogating witnesses and presenting evidence so as to (1) make the interrogation and presentation effective for the ascertainment of the truth, (2) avoid needless consumption of time, and (3) protect witnesses from harassment or undue embarrassment.

(b) **Scope of cross-examination**. Cross-examination should be limited to the subject matter of the direct examination and matters affecting the credibility of the witness. The court may, in the exercise of discretion, permit inquiry into additional matters as if on direct examination.

(c) **Leading questions**. Leading questions should not be used on the direct examination of a witness except as may be necessary to develop the witness' testimony. Ordinarily, leading questions should be permitted on cross-examination. When a party calls a hostile witness, an adverse party, or a witness identified with an adverse party, interrogation may be by leading questions.

Rule 612. Writing used to refresh memory.

If a witness uses a writing to refresh the witness' memory for the purpose of testifying, either:

(1)   While testifying, or

(2)   Before testifying, if the court in its discretion determines it is necessary in the interests of justice,

an adverse party is entitled to have the writing produced at the hearing, to inspect it, to cross-examine the witness thereon, and to introduce in evidence those portions which relate to the testimony of the witness. If it is claimed that the writing contains matters not related to the subject matter of the testimony the court shall examine the writing in camera, excise any portions not so related, and order delivery of the remainder to the party entitled thereto. Any portion withheld over objections shall be preserved and made available to the appellate court in the event of an appeal. If a writing is not produced or delivered pursuant to order under this rule, the court shall make any order justice requires, except that in criminal cases when the prosecution elects not to comply, the order shall be one striking the testimony or, if the court in its discretion determines that the interests of justice so require, declaring a mistrial.

Rule 613. Prior statements of witnesses.

(a)   **Examining witness concerning prior statement**. In examining a witness concerning a prior statement made by the witness, whether written or not, the statement need not be shown nor its contents disclosed to the witness at that time, but on request the same shall be shown or disclosed to opposing counsel.

(b)   **Extrinsic evidence of prior inconsistent statement of witness**. Extrinsic evidence of a prior inconsistent statement by a witness is not admissible unless, on direct or cross-examination, (1) the circumstances of the statement have been brought to the attention of the witness, and (2) the witness has been asked whether the witness made the statement.

(c)   **Prior consistent statement of witness**. Evidence of a statement previously made by a witness that is consistent with the witness' testimony at the trial is admissible to support the witness' credibility only if it is offered after:

(1)   Evidence of the witness' prior inconsistent statement has been admitted for the purpose of attacking the witness' credibility, and the consistent statement was made before the inconsistent statement; or

(2)   An express or implied charge has been made that the witness' testimony at the trial is recently fabricated or is

influenced by bias or other improper motive, and the
consistent statement was made before the bias, motive for
fabrication, or other improper motive is alleged to have
arisen; or

(3)   The witness' credibility has been attacked at the trial by
imputation of inaccurate memory, and the consistent
statement was made when the event was recent and the
witness' memory fresh.

Rule 614. Calling and interrogation of witness by court.

(a) **Calling by court**. The court may, on its own motion or at the
suggestion of a party, call witnesses, and all parties are entitled to
cross-examine witnesses thus called.
(b) **Interrogation by court**. The court may interrogate witnesses,
whether called by itself or by a party.
(c) **Objections**. Objections to the calling of witnesses by the court or to
interrogation by it may be made at the time or at the next available
opportunity when the jury is not present.

Rule 615. Exclusion of witnesses.

At the request of a party the court shall order witnesses excluded so that
they cannot hear the testimony of other witnesses, and it may make the
order of its own motion. This rule does not authorize exclusion of (1) a
party who is a natural person, or (2) an officer or employee of a party
which is not a natural person designated as its representative by its
attorney, or (3) a person whose presence is shown by a party to be
essential to the presentation of the party's cause.

Rule 616. Televised testimony of child.

In any prosecution of an abuse offense or sexual offense alleged to
have been committed against a child less than eighteen years of age at
the time of the testimony, the court may order that the testimony of the
child be taken in a room other than the courtroom and be televised by
two-way closed circuit video equipment to be viewed by the court, the
accused, and the trier of fact, if the court finds that requiring the child
to testify in the physical presence of the accused would likely result in
serious emotional distress to the child and substantial impairment of the
child's ability to communicate. During the entire course of such a
procedure, the attorneys for the defendant and for the State shall have
the right to be present with the child, and full direct and cross-
examination shall be available as a matter of right.

Rule 616. Televised testimony of child.

Article VII - Opinions and Expert Testimony

Rule 701. Opinion testimony by lay witnesses.

If the witness is not testifying as an expert, the witness' testimony in the form of opinions or inferences is limited to those opinions or inferences which are (1) rationally based on the perception of the witness, and (2) helpful to a clear understanding of the witness' testimony or the determination of a fact in issue.

Rule 702. Testimony by experts.

If scientific, technical, or other specialized knowledge will assist the trier of fact to understand the evidence or to determine a fact in issue, a witness qualified as an expert by knowledge, skill, experience, training, or education may testify thereto in the form of an opinion or otherwise. In determining the issue of assistance to the trier of fact, the court may consider the trustworthiness and validity of the scientific technique or mode of analysis employed by the proffered expert.

Rule 702.1. Cross-examination of experts.

(a) **General**. A witness testifying as an expert may be cross-examined to the same extent as any other witness and, in addition, may be cross-examined as to (1) the witness' qualifications, (2) the subject to which the witness' expert testimony relates, and (3) the matter upon which the witness' opinion is based and the reasons for the witness' opinion.
(b) **Texts and treatises**. If a witness testifying as an expert testifies in the form of an opinion, the witness may be cross-examined in regard to the content or tenor of any scientific, technical, or professional text, treatise, journal, or similar publication only if:
    (1)   The witness referred to, considered, or relied upon such publication in arriving at or forming the witness' opinion, or
    (2)   Such publication qualifies for admission into evidence under rule 803(b)(18).

Rule 703. Bases of opinion testimony by experts.

The facts or data in the particular case upon which an expert bases an opinion or inference may be those perceived by or made known to the expert at or before the hearing. If of a type reasonably relied upon by experts in the particular field in forming opinions or inferences upon the subject, the facts or data need not be admissible in evidence. The court may, however, disallow testimony in the form of an opinion or inference if the underlying facts or data indicate lack of trustworthiness.

Rule 704. Opinion on ultimate issue.

Testimony in the form of an opinion or inference otherwise admissible is not objectionable because it embraces an ultimate issue to be decided by the trier of fact.

Rule 705. Disclosure of facts or data underlying expert opinion.

The expert may testify in terms of opinion or inference and give the expert's reasons therefor without disclosing the underlying facts or data if the underlying facts or data have been disclosed in discovery proceedings. The expert may in any event be required to disclose the underlying facts or data on cross-examination.

Rule 706. Court-appointed experts.

In the exercise of its discretion, the court may authorize disclosure to the jury of the fact that a particular expert witness was appointed by the court.

Article VIII - Hearsay

Rule 801. Definitions.

The following definitions apply under this article:
- (1) "Declarant" is a person who makes a statement.
- (2) "Hearsay" is a statement, other than one made by the declarant while testifying at the trial or hearing, offered in evidence to prove the truth of the matter asserted.
- (3) "Statement" is an oral assertion, an assertion in a writing, or nonverbal conduct of a person, if it is intended by the person as an assertion.

Rule 802. Hearsay rule.

Hearsay is not admissible except as provided by these rules, or by other rules prescribed by the Hawaii supreme court, or by statute.

Rule 802.1. Hearsay exception; prior statements by witnesses.

The following statements previously made by witnesses who testify at the trial or hearing are not excluded by the hearsay rule:
- (1) **Inconsistent statement**. The declarant is subject to cross-examination concerning the subject matter of the declarant's statement, the statement is inconsistent with the declarant's testimony, the statement is offered in compliance with rule 613(b), and the statement was:
    - (A) Given under oath subject to the penalty of perjury at a trial, hearing, or other proceeding, or in a deposition; or
    - (B) Reduced to writing and signed or otherwise adopted or approved by the declarant; or
    - (C) Recorded in substantially verbatim fashion by stenographic, mechanical, electrical, or other means contemporaneously with the making of the statement;
- (2) **Consistent statement**. The declarant is subject to cross-examination concerning the subject matter of the declarant's statement, the statement is consistent with the declarant's testimony, and the statement is offered in compliance with rule 613(c);
- (3) **Prior identification**. The declarant is subject to cross-examination concerning the subject matter of the declarant's

statement, and the statement is one of identification of a person made after perceiving that person; or

(4) **Past recollection recorded**. A memorandum or record concerning a matter about which the witness once had knowledge but now has insufficient recollection to enable the witness to testify fully and accurately, shown to have been made or adopted by the witness when the matter was fresh in the witness' memory and to reflect that knowledge correctly. If admitted, the memorandum or record may be read into evidence but may not itself be received as an exhibit unless offered by an adverse party.

Rule 803. Hearsay exceptions; availability of declarant immaterial.

The following are not excluded by the hearsay rule, even though the declarant is available as a witness:

(a) **Admissions**.

(1) *Admission by party-opponent*. A statement that is offered against a party and is (A) the party's own statement, in either the party's individual or a representative capacity, or (B) a statement of which the party has manifested the party's adoption or belief in its truth.

(2) *Vicarious admissions*. A statement that is offered against a party and was uttered by (A) a person authorized by the party to make such a statement, (B) the party's agent or servant concerning a matter within the scope of the agent's or servant's agency or employment, made during the existence of the relationship, or (C) a co-conspirator of the party during the course and in furtherance of the conspiracy.

(3) *Admission by deceased in wrongful death action*. A statement by the deceased, offered against the plaintiff in an action for the wrongful death of that deceased.

(4) *Admission by predecessor in interest*. When a right, title, or interest in any property or claim asserted by a party to a civil action requires a determination that a right, title, or interest exists or existed in the declarant, evidence of a statement made by the declarant during the time the party now claims the declarant was the holder of the right, title, or interest is as admissible against the party as it would be if offered against the declarant in an action involving that right, title, or interest.

(5) *Admission by predecessor in litigation*. When the liability, obligation, or duty of a party to a civil action is based in

whole or in part upon the liability, obligation, or duty of the declarant, or when the claim or right asserted by a party to a civil action is barred or diminished by a breach of duty by the declarant, evidence of a statement made by the declarant is as admissible against the party as it would be if offered against the declarant in an action involving that liability, obligation, duty, or breach of duty.

(b) **Other exceptions**.

    (1) *Present sense impression.* A statement describing or explaining an event or condition made while the declarant was perceiving the event or condition or immediately thereafter.

    (2) *Excited utterance.* A statement relating to a startling event or condition made while the declarant was under the stress of excitement caused by the event or condition.

    (3) *Then existing mental, emotional, or physical condition.* A statement of the declarant's then existing state of mind, emotion, sensation, or physical condition (such as intent, plan, motive, design, mental feeling, pain, and bodily health), but not including a statement of memory or belief to prove the fact remembered or believed unless it relates to the execution, revocation, identification, or terms of declarant's will.

    (4) *Statements for purposes of medical diagnosis or treatment.* Statements made for purposes of medical diagnosis or treatment and describing medical history, or past or present symptoms, pain, or sensations, or the inception or general character of the cause or external source thereof insofar as reasonably pertinent to diagnosis or treatment.

    (5) *Reserved.*

    (6) *Records of regularly conducted activity.* A memorandum, report, record, or data compilation, in any form, of acts, events, conditions, opinions, or diagnoses, made in the course of a regularly conducted activity, at or near the time of the acts, events, conditions, opinions, or diagnoses, as shown by the testimony of the custodian or other qualified witness, or by certification that complies with rule 902(11) or a statute permitting certification, unless the sources of information or other circumstances indicate lack of trustworthiness.

    (7) *Absence of entry in records kept in accordance with the provisions of paragraph (6).* Evidence that a matter is not included in the memoranda, reports, records, or data

compilations, in any form, kept in accordance with the provisions of paragraph (6), to prove the nonoccurrence or nonexistence of the matter, if the matter was of a kind of which a memorandum, report, record, or data compilation was regularly made and preserved, unless the sources of information or other circumstances indicate lack of trustworthiness.

(8) *Public records and reports.* Records, reports, statements, or data compilations, in any form, of public offices or agencies, setting forth (A) the activities of the office or agency, or (B) matters observed pursuant to duty imposed by law as to which matters there was a duty to report, excluding, however, in criminal cases matters observed by police officers and other law enforcement personnel, or (C) in civil proceedings and against the government in criminal cases, factual findings resulting from an investigation made pursuant to authority granted by law, unless the sources of information or other circumstances indicate lack of trustworthiness.

(9) *Records of vital statistics.* Records or data compilations, in any form, of births, fetal deaths, deaths, or marriages, if the report thereof was made to a public office pursuant to requirements of law.

(10) *Absence of public record or entry.* To prove the absence of a record, report, statement, or data compilation, in any form, or the nonoccurrence or nonexistence of a matter of which a record, report, statement, or data compilation, in any form, was regularly made and preserved by a public office or agency, evidence in the form of a certification in accordance with rule 902, or testimony, that diligent search failed to disclose the record, report, statement, or data compilation, or entry.

(11) *Records of religious organizations.* Statements of births, marriages, divorces, deaths, legitimacy, ancestry, relationship by blood or marriage, or other similar facts of personal or family history, contained in a regularly kept record of a religious organization.

(12) *Marriage, baptismal, and similar certificates.* Statements of fact contained in a certificate that the maker performed a marriage or other ceremony or administered a sacrament, made by a clergyman, public official, or other person authorized by the rules or practices of a religious organization or by law to perform the act certified, and

purporting to have been issued at the time of the act or within a reasonable time thereafter.

(13) *Family records.* Statements of fact concerning personal or family history contained in family Bibles, genealogies, charts, engravings on rings, inscriptions on family portraits, engravings on urns, crypts, or tombstones, or the like.

(14) *Records of documents affecting an interest in property.* The record of a document purporting to establish or affect an interest in property, as proof of the content of the original recorded document and its execution and delivery by each person by whom it purports to have been executed, if the record is a record of a public office and an applicable statute authorizes the recording of documents of that kind in that office.

(15) *Statements in documents affecting an interest in property.* A statement contained in a document purporting to establish or affect an interest in property if the matter stated was relevant to the purpose of the document, unless the circumstances indicate lack of trustworthiness.

(16) *Statements in ancient documents.* Statements in a document in existence twenty years or more the authenticity of which is established.

(17) *Market reports, commercial publications.* Market quotations, tabulations, lists, directories, or other published compilations, generally used and relied upon by the public or by persons in particular occupations.

(18) *Learned treatises.* To the extent called to the attention of an expert witness upon cross-examination or relied upon by the witness in direct examination, statements contained in published treatises, periodicals, or pamphlets on a subject of history, medicine, or other science or art, established as a reliable authority by the testimony or admission of the witness or by other expert testimony or by judicial notice. If admitted, the statements may be read into evidence but may not be received as exhibits.

(19) *Reputation concerning personal or family history.* Reputation among members of the person's family by blood, adoption, or marriage, or among the person's associates, or in the community, concerning a person's birth, adoption, marriage, divorce, death, legitimacy, relationship by blood, adoption, or marriage, ancestry, or other similar fact of the person's personal or family history.

(20) *Reputation concerning boundaries or general history.* Reputation in a community, arising before the controversy, as to boundaries of or customs affecting lands in the community, and reputation as to events of general history important to the community or state or nation in which located.

(21) *Reputation as to character.* In proving character or a trait of character under rules 404 and 405, reputation of a person's character among the person's associates or in the community.

(22) *Judgment of previous conviction.* Evidence of a final judgment, entered after a trial or upon a plea of guilty (but not upon a plea of nolo contendere), adjudging a person guilty of a crime punishable by death or imprisonment in excess of one year, to prove any fact essential to sustain the judgment, but not including, when offered by the government in a criminal prosecution for purposes other than impeachment, judgments against persons other than the accused. The pendency of an appeal may be shown but does not affect admissibility.

(23) *Judgment as to personal, family or general history, or boundaries.* Judgments as proof of matters of personal, family or general history, or boundaries, essential to the judgment, if the same would be provable by evidence of reputation.

(24) *Other exceptions.* A statement not specifically covered by any of the exceptions in this paragraph (b) but having equivalent circumstantial guarantees of trustworthiness, if the court determines that (A) the statement is more probative on the point for which it is offered than any other evidence which the proponent can procure through reasonable efforts, and (B) the general purposes of these rules and the interests of justice will best be served by admission of the statement into evidence. However, a statement may not be admitted under this exception unless the proponent of it makes known to the adverse party sufficiently in advance of the trial or hearing to provide the adverse party with a fair opportunity to prepare to meet it, the proponent's intention to offer the statement and the particulars of it, including the name and address of the declarant.

Rule 804. Hearsay exceptions; declarant unavailable.

(a) **Definition of unavailability**. "Unavailability as a witness" includes situations in which the declarant:

    (1) Is exempted by ruling of the court on the ground of privilege from testifying concerning the subject matter of the declarant's statement;

    (2) Persists in refusing to testify concerning the subject matter of the declarant's statement despite an order of the court to do so;

    (3) Testifies to a lack of memory of the subject matter of the declarant's statement;

    (4) Is unable to be present or to testify at the hearing because of death or then existing physical or mental illness or infirmity; or

    (5) Is absent from the hearing and the proponent of the declarant's statement has been unable to procure the declarant's attendance by process or other reasonable means.

A declarant is not unavailable as a witness if the declarant's exemption, refusal, claim of lack of memory, inability, or absence is due to the procurement or wrongdoing of the proponent of the declarant's statement for the purpose of preventing the witness from attending or testifying. Determination of unavailability as a witness pursuant to this rule does not affect the opponent's right, under rule 806, to call and to cross-examine the declarant concerning the subject matter of any statement received in accordance with this rule.

(b) **Hearsay exceptions**. The following are not excluded by the hearsay rule if the declarant is unavailable as a witness:

    (1) *Former testimony*. Testimony given as a witness at another hearing of the same or a different proceeding, or in a deposition taken in compliance with law in the course of the same or another proceeding, at the instance of or against a party with an opportunity to develop the testimony by direct, cross, or redirect examination, with motive and interest similar to those of the party against whom now offered;

    (2) *Statement under belief of impending death*. A statement made by a declarant while believing that the declarant's death was imminent, concerning the cause or circumstances of what the declarant believed to be the declarant's impending death;

    (3) *Statement against interest*. A statement which was at the time of its making so far contrary to the declarant's pecuniary or proprietary interest, or so far tended to subject

the declarant to civil or criminal liability, or to render invalid a claim by the declarant against another, that a reasonable person in the declarant's position would not have made the statement unless the declarant believed it to be true. A statement tending to expose the declarant to criminal liability and offered to exculpate the accused is not admissible unless corroborating circumstances clearly indicate the trustworthiness of the statement;

(4) *Statement of personal or family history.* (A) A statement concerning the declarant's own birth, adoption, marriage, divorce, legitimacy, relationship by blood, adoption, or marriage, ancestry, or other similar fact of personal or family history, even though declarant had no means of acquiring personal knowledge of the matter stated; or (B) a statement concerning the foregoing matters, and death also, of another person, if the declarant was related to the other by blood, adoption, or marriage or was so intimately associated with the other's family as to be likely to have accurate information concerning the matter declared;

(5) *Statement of recent perception.* A statement, not in response to the instigation of a person engaged in investigating, litigating, or settling a claim, which narrates, describes, or explains an event or condition recently perceived by the declarant, made in good faith, not in contemplation of pending or anticipated litigation in which the declarant was interested, and while the declarant's recollection was clear;

(6) *Statement by child.* A statement made by a child when under the age of sixteen, describing any act of sexual contact, sexual penetration, or physical violence performed with or against the child by another, if the court determines that the time, content, and circumstances of the statement provide strong assurances of trustworthiness with regard to appropriate factors that include but are not limited to: (A) age and mental condition of the declarant; (B) spontaneity and absence of suggestion; (C) appropriateness of the language and terminology of the statement, given the child's age; (D) lack of motive to fabricate; (E) time interval between the event and the statement, and the reasons therefor; and (F) whether or not the statement was recorded, and the time, circumstances, and method of the recording. If admitted, the statement may be read or, in the event of a recorded statement, broadcast into evidence but may not

itself be received as an exhibit unless offered by an adverse party;

(7) *Forfeiture by wrongdoing.* A statement offered against a party that has procured the unavailability of the declarant as a witness;

(8) *Other exceptions.* A statement not specifically covered by any of the foregoing exceptions but having equivalent circumstantial guarantees of trustworthiness, if the court determines that (A) the statement is more probative on the point for which it is offered than any other evidence which the proponent can procure through reasonable efforts, and (B) the general purposes of these rules and the interests of justice will best be served by admission of the statement into evidence. However, a statement may not be admitted under this exception unless the proponent of it makes known to the adverse party sufficiently in advance of the trial or hearing to provide the adverse party with a fair opportunity to prepare to meet it, the proponent's intention to offer the statement and the particulars of it, including the name and address of the declarant.

Rule 805. Hearsay within hearsay.

Hearsay included within hearsay is not excluded under the hearsay rule if each part of the combined statements conforms with an exception to the hearsay rule provided in these rules.

Rule 806. Attacking and supporting credibility of declarant.

When a hearsay statement has been admitted in evidence, the credibility of the declarant may be attacked, and if attacked may be supported, by any evidence which would be admissible for those purposes if declarant had testified as a witness. Evidence of a statement or conduct by the declarant at any time, inconsistent with the declarant's hearsay statement, is not subject to any requirement that the declarant may have been afforded an opportunity to deny or explain. If the party against whom a hearsay statement has been admitted calls the declarant as a witness, the party is entitled to examine the declarant on the statement as if under cross-examination.

Rule 806. Attacking and supporting credibility of declarant.

Article IX - Authentication and Identification

Rule 901. Requirement of authentication or identification.

(a) **General provision**. The requirement of authentication or identification as a condition precedent to admissibility is satisfied by evidence sufficient to support a finding that the matter in question is what its proponent claims.

(b) **Illustrations**. By way of illustration only, and not by way of limitation, the following are examples of authentication or identification conforming with the requirements of this rule:

    (1) *Testimony of witness with knowledge*. Testimony that a matter is what it is claimed to be.

    (2) *Nonexpert opinion on handwriting*. Nonexpert opinion as to the genuineness of handwriting, based upon familiarity not acquired for purposes of the litigation.

    (3) *Comparison by trier or expert witness*. Comparison by the trier of fact or by expert witnesses with specimens which have been authenticated.

    (4) *Distinctive characteristics and the like*. Appearance, contents, substance, internal patterns, or other distinctive characteristics, taken in conjunction with circumstances.

    (5) *Voice identification*. Identification of a voice, whether heard firsthand or through mechanical or electronic transmission or recording, by opinion based upon hearing the voice at any time under circumstances connecting it with the alleged speaker.

    (6) *Telephone conversations*. Telephone conversations, by evidence that a call was made to the number assigned at the time by the telephone company to a particular person or business, if (A) in the case of a person, circumstances, including self-identification, show the person answering to be the one called, or (B) in the case of a business, the call was made to a place of business and the conversation related to business reasonably transacted over the telephone.

    (7) *Public records or reports*. Evidence that a writing authorized by law to be recorded or filed and in fact recorded or filed in a public office, or a purported public record, report, statement, or data compilation, in any form, is from the public office where items of this nature are kept.

    (8) *Ancient documents or data compilation*. Evidence that a document or data compilation, in any form, (A) is in such condition as to create no suspicion concerning its authenticity, (B) was in a place where it, if authentic, would

likely be, and (C) has been in existence twenty years or more at the time it is offered.

(9) *Process or system.* Evidence describing a process or system used to produce a result and showing that the process or system produces an accurate result.

(10) *Methods provided by statute or rule.* Any method of authentication or identification provided by statute or by other rules prescribed by the supreme court.

Rule 902. Self-authentication.

Extrinsic evidence of authenticity as a condition precedent to admissibility is not required with respect to the following:

(1) *Domestic public documents under seal.* A document bearing a seal purporting to be that of the United States, or of any state, district, commonwealth, territory, or insular possession thereof, or the Panama Canal Zone, or the Trust Territory of the Pacific Islands, or of a political subdivision, department, officer, or agency thereof, and a signature purporting to be an attestation or execution.

(2) *Domestic public documents not under seal.* A document purporting to bear the signature in the official capacity of an officer or employee of any entity included in paragraph (1), having no seal, if a public officer having a seal and having official duties in the district or political subdivision of the officer or employee certifies under seal that the signer has the official capacity and that the signature is genuine.

(3) *Foreign public documents.* A document purporting to be executed or attested in an official capacity by a person authorized by the laws of a foreign country to make the execution or attestation, and accompanied by a final certification as to the genuineness of the signature and official position (A) of the executing or attesting person, or (B) of any foreign official whose certificate of genuineness of signature and official position relates to the execution or attestation or is in a chain of certificates of genuineness of signature and official position relating to the execution or attestation. A final certification may be made by a secretary of embassy or legation, consul general, consul, vice consul, or consular agent of the United States, or a diplomatic or consular official of the foreign country assigned or accredited to the United States. If reasonable opportunity has been given to all parties to investigate the authenticity and accuracy of official documents, the court may, for good

cause shown, order that they be treated as presumptively authentic without final certification or permit them to be evidenced by an attested summary with or without final certification.

(4) *Certified copies of public records.* A copy of an official record or report or entry therein, or of a document authorized by law to be recorded or filed and actually recorded or filed in a public office, including data compilations in any form, certified as correct by the custodian or other person authorized to make the certification, by certificate complying with paragraph (1), (2), or (3) or complying with any statute or rule prescribed by the supreme court.

(5) *Official publications.* Books, pamphlets, or other publications purporting to be issued by public authority.

(6) *Newspapers and periodicals.* Printed materials purporting to be newspapers or periodicals.

(7) *Trade inscriptions and the like.* Inscriptions, signs, tags, or labels purporting to have been affixed in the course of business and indicating ownership, control, or origin.

(8) *Acknowledged documents.* Documents accompanied by a certificate of acknowledgment executed in the manner provided by law by a notary public or other officer authorized by law to take acknowledgments.

(9) *Commercial paper and related documents.* Commercial paper, signatures thereon, and documents relating thereto to the extent provided by general commercial law.

(10) *Presumptions under statutes.* Any signature, document, or other matter declared by statute to be presumptively or prima facie genuine or authentic.

(11) *Certified records of regularly conducted activity.* The original or a duplicate of a domestic or foreign record of regularly conducted activity that would be admissible under rule 803(b)(6), if accompanied by a written declaration of its custodian or other qualified person, certifying that the record was:

    (A)   Made at or near the time of the occurrence of the matters set forth by, or from information transmitted by, a person with knowledge of those matters;

    (B)   Kept in the course of the regularly conducted activity; and

    (C)   Made by the regularly conducted activity as a regular practice.

The declaration shall be signed in a manner that, if falsely made, would subject the maker to a criminal penalty under the laws of the state or country where the declaration is signed. A party intending to offer a record into evidence under this paragraph shall provide reasonable notice in advance of trial, or during trial if the court excuses pretrial notice on good cause shown, of that intention to all adverse parties, and shall make the record and declaration available for inspection sufficiently in advance of their offer into evidence to provide an adverse party with a fair opportunity to challenge them.

Rule 903. Subscribing witness' testimony unnecessary.

The testimony of a subscribing witness is not necessary to authenticate a writing.

Article X - Contents of Writings, Recordings, and Photographs

Rule 1001. Definitions.

For purposes of this article the following definitions are applicable:

(1) "Writings and recordings" consist of letters, words, sounds, or numbers, or their equivalent, set down by handwriting, typewriting, printing, photostating, photographing, magnetic impulse, mechanical or electronic recording, or other form of data compilation.

(2) "Photographs" include still photographs, X-ray films, video tapes, and motion pictures.

(3) An "original" of a writing or recording is the writing or recording itself or any counterpart intended to have the same effect by a person executing or issuing it. An "original" of a photograph includes the negative or any print therefrom. If data are stored in a computer or similar device, any printout or other output readable by sight, shown to reflect the data accurately, is an "original".

(4) A "duplicate" is a counterpart produced by the same impression as the original, or from the same matrix, or by means of photography, including enlargements and miniatures, or by mechanical or electronic re-recording, or by chemical reproduction, or by other equivalent techniques which accurately reproduce the original.

(5) A "public record" means any writing, memorandum, entry, print, representation, report, book or paper, map or plan, or combination thereof, that is in the custody of any department or agency of government.

Rule 1002. Requirement of original.

To prove the content of a writing, recording, or photograph, the original writing, recording, or photograph is required, except as otherwise provided in these rules or by statute.

Rule 1003. Admissibility of duplicates.

A duplicate is admissible to the same extent as an original unless (1) a genuine question is raised as to the authenticity of the original, or (2) in the circumstances it would be unfair to admit the duplicate in lieu of the original.

Rule 1004. Admissibility of other evidence of contents.

The original or a duplicate is not required, and other evidence of the contents of a writing, recording, or photograph is admissible if:

(1) *Originals lost or destroyed.* All originals are lost or have been destroyed, unless the proponent lost or destroyed them in bad faith; or

(2) *Original not obtainable.* No original can be obtained by available judicial process or procedure; or

(3) *Original in possession of opponent.* At a time when an original was under the control of the party against whom offered, the party was put on notice, by the pleadings or otherwise, that the content would be a subject of proof at the hearing, and the party does not produce the original at the hearing; or

(4) *Collateral matters.* The writing, recording, or photograph is not closely related to a controlling issue.

Rule 1005. Public records.

The contents of a public record, if otherwise admissible, may be proved by copy, certified as correct in accordance with rule 902 or testified to be correct by a witness who has compared it with the original. If a copy which complies with the foregoing cannot be obtained by the exercise of reasonable diligence, then other evidence of the contents may be given.

Rule 1006. Summaries.

The contents of voluminous writings, recordings, or photographs which cannot conveniently be examined in court may be presented in the form of a chart, summary, or calculation. The originals, or duplicates, shall be made available for examination or copying, or both, by other parties at reasonable time and place. The court may order that they be produced in court.

Rule 1007. Testimony or written admission of party.

Contents of writings, recordings, or photographs may be proved by the testimony or deposition of the party against whom offered or by the party's written admission, without accounting for the nonproduction of the original.

Rule 1008. Functions of court and jury.

When the admissibility of other evidence of contents of writings, recordings, or photographs under these rules depends upon the fulfillment of a condition of fact, the question whether the condition has been fulfilled is ordinarily for the court to determine in accordance with the provisions of rule 104. However, when an issue is raised (1) whether the asserted writing ever existed, or (2) whether another writing, recording, or photograph produced at the trial is the original, or (3) whether other evidence of contents correctly reflects the contents, the issue is for the trier of fact to determine as in the case of other issues of fact.

Rule 1008. Functions of court and jury.

Article XII - Miscellaneous Rules

Rule 1101 Applicability of rules.

(a) **Courts**. These rules apply to all courts of the State of Hawaii except as otherwise provided by statute.

(b) **Proceedings**. These rules apply generally to civil and criminal proceedings.

(c) **Rule of privilege**. The rule with respect to privileges applies at all stages of all actions, cases, and proceedings.

(d) **Rules inapplicable**. The rules (other than with respect to privileges) do not apply in the following:

    (1) *Preliminary questions of fact*. The determination of questions of fact preliminary to admissibility of evidence when the issue is to be determined by the court under rule 104.

    (2) *Grand jury*. Proceedings before grand juries.

    (3) *Miscellaneous proceedings*. Proceedings for extradition or rendition; preliminary hearings in criminal cases; sentencing, or granting or revoking probation; issuance of warrants for arrest, criminal summonses, and search warrants; and proceedings with respect to release on bail or otherwise.

    (4) *Small claims*. Proceedings before the small claims division of the district courts.

Rule 1102 Jury instructions; comment on evidence prohibited.

The court shall instruct the jury regarding the law applicable to the facts of the case, but shall not comment upon the evidence. It shall also inform the jury that they are the exclusive judges of all questions of fact and the credibility of witnesses.